Our **WILD**™ **WORLD** SERIES

Owls

Text and Photographs by Wayne Lynch
Illustrations by Sherry Neidigh

NORTHWORD PRESS
Minnetonka, Minnesota

WORLDWIDE, THERE ARE OVER 200 kinds, or species (SPEE-sees), of owls. Most live in the dense forests of the hot tropics, and only 19 are found in the United States and Canada. Among these owls is the smallest owl in the world, the elf owl. Another one, the snowy owl, is one of the heaviest and most powerful owls in the world.

The elf owl is no larger than a house sparrow and it would take 60 elf owls to weigh as much as the snowy owl of the Arctic. Just one feather from the end of a snowy's wing is twice as tall as a tiny elf owl. In fact, a hungry snowy owl could gulp down a dozen elf owls for lunch and still be hungry for more.

Owls are found in every corner of the United States and Canada. They live in the deserts of the Southwest, the grasslands of the prairies, and on the Arctic tundra of Alaska. They also live in the Rocky Mountains, in the dark spruce forests of Canada, in the cypress swamps of Florida and Louisiana, and in the forests of New England.

If you love owls, the best places to live are in Washington and British Columbia—each is home to 14 different owl species.

An adult female snowy owl may weigh more than 5 pounds (2.25 kilograms).

The feather ear tufts on a great horned owl have nothing to do with hearing. The bird uses them for display.

In the past, owls were a frequent part of human customs and beliefs. Cherokee Indians believed if you washed a newborn baby's eyes with water in which an owl's feather had been soaked, the child would see better at night. In Europe, people nailed a dead owl over their front door to protect the family from disease. They sometimes killed a second owl and hung its body on their barn to guard against heavy rain, hail, and lightning storms. For many in Europe, an owl was a feathered witch that could forecast the weather, warn of death, or kidnap naughty children.

Today, many people believe it is bad luck to have an owl fly over them. The funniest story about owls claims that if you walk around an owl many times in one direction the bird will twist off its own head! Of course, all of these stories and beliefs are untrue, and the real story about owls is better than any fairy tale.

Owls
FUNFACT:

A group of owls is called a parliament (PAR-luh-ment).

During the day, the western screech owl hides from predators in the thick branches of a tree or bush.

The thick, strong talons on a great horned owl may be almost 1 inch (2.5 centimeters) long.

Owls, like hawks and eagles, are birds of prey (PRAY), or raptors (RAP-torz). They attack, kill, and eat other animals for their food. To do this they need weapons, and an owl's beak and feet are deadly weapons. The beak on all owls is hooked and has razor-sharp edges designed for killing and cutting. Each of the bird's feet has 4 needle-sharp claws, called talons. The feet of many northern owls, such as the great horned, great gray, boreal, and snowy owl, are covered with thick feathers to protect them from the snow and cold of long winters.

Most owls hunt and move around in the darkness. In the daytime, they quietly hide in buildings, bushes, hollow trees, or on branches surrounded by thick greenery. The body feathers on most owls are shades of gray and brown to help them blend into the shadows of their hiding places.

For example, the feather pattern on an eastern or western screech owl looks like the scaly bark on a tree. When these small owls huddle next to a tree trunk, it is almost impossible to see them.

By hunting at night, owls avoid competing with daytime hunters such as hawks, falcons, and eagles. They also lessen their chances of being eaten by these hungry raptors.

In winter, when temperatures are cold, the eastern screech owl may snooze in the sunshine during the day to warm itself.

Long-eared owls normally hunt only at night, but they may hunt in the middle of the day.

It is not easy for birds to fly in darkness. To help owls fly at night they have very large eyes. The eyes of a great horned owl are the largest of any owl in North America, and as big as an adult human's eye. Large eyes produce a large picture on the back of the eyeball, and a large picture has more details in it than a small one.

Also, the pupil in an owl's eye is very big. The pupil is the black circle in the center of the eye. A large pupil lets more light into the eye than a small pupil does. It works in the same way that a large window lets more sunlight into a room than a small window.

Owls can also focus their eyes very quickly. This helps them to see branches clearly when they are flying swiftly through a forest at night.

Owls may also memorize the location and pattern of the trees in the forest where they live. Since an owl may hunt in the same forest for months, and sometimes years, it learns where it can fly safely so it does not bump into anything. Many nighttime forest owls also hunt in nearby fields and marshes where there are no trees to worry about.

Even if an owl can fly safely at night, it's an even bigger job to find and catch a tiny mouse on a dark forest floor. Animals that are active at night are called nocturnal (nok-TURN-ul). Nocturnal owls depend on their sensitive hearing, as well as their good eyesight, to locate and catch their meals.

Owls have better hearing than any other group of birds. The owls that hear the best are those that live where deep snow covers the ground in winter. These owls, such as the great gray, the northern saw-whet, and the boreal owl, rely on their sensitive ears to hear voles, lemmings, and mice running and squeaking underneath the snow. A great gray owl can hear a vole hidden under as much as 18 inches (46 centimeters) of snow!

Some people have claimed that nocturnal owls can see 100 times better than humans in the dark, and that they can hear much better than we can as well. This is not true. Recent scientific studies have proven that no owl hears as well as the average human. In fact, some humans hear better than owls.

However, owls see better than we do at night, but only 2 or 3 times better, not 100 times. Because we depend so much on lights to guide us at night we rarely have a chance to test our nocturnal vision.

If you were to go into a forest at night and sit for 40 minutes in the darkness, your eyes would slowly adjust to the dim light from the moon and the stars. In the end, surprisingly, you would see almost as well as an owl. Try it sometime!

Owls
FUNFACT:

The snowy owl of the Arctic has the warmest coat of feathers of any bird of prey. It stays warm even when the temperature is –40 degrees Fahrenheit (–40 degrees Celcius).

The long tail on the northern hawk owl allows it to make quick turns, which is helpful when it hunts birds.

In winter, many arctic snowy owls move to the Canadian prairies where they hunt in old wheat fields.

Although most owls in the United States and Canada are nocturnal, at least six species are diurnal (die-YER-nul), which means they hunt in the daytime, or crepuscular (krip-US-kyoo-ler), which means they hunt at dusk and dawn. The great gray owl, northern hawk owl, snowy owl and northern pygmy-owl are good examples of owls that are diurnal and crepuscular. All of them live in northern forests or the Arctic where the nights are very short in the summer.

Most owls use the perch-and-pounce style of hunting. They quietly sit on a branch, a ledge, or a telephone pole and wait for some careless animal to flutter, scurry, or squeak and then they swoop down on it. A hunting boreal owl may perch only 6 feet (1.8 meters) off the ground, watch and listen for two or three minutes, then fly to another perch and start again if there are no prey animals in the area. The owl may do this for many hours each night.

The soft feathers of a barred owl help it to fly quietly and catch mice even though mice have excellent hearing.

Some owls use other ways to catch their meals. The long-eared and short-eared owls hunt in open spaces, such as meadows and marshes, where they fly slowly back and forth, close to the ground. The great horned owl and the northern hawk owl sometimes flap-and-glide through open woods, hoping to frighten an animal and make it run from its hiding place.

Flying quietly is important if a hunting owl is to succeed. It needs to be quiet for two reasons. First, an owl always wants to attack by surprise. Any sound might warn the prey and give it time to escape. Second, noisy wings make it difficult for an owl to hear the faint sounds of its prey in the snow or grass.

If you open a car window while driving along the highway, you immediately notice the noise of the wind and how much more difficult it is to hear conversation. The noise is called turbulence (TER-bu-lence). To prevent turbulence when they fly, many owls have a fine feathery fringe along the front and rear edges of their wings. This muffles the noise of their flight. They also have soft fuzz on the surface of their wing feathers to prevent noise when the feathers rub against each other.

Owl wings are very large for the size of the bird and this also helps the birds to fly silently, especially when taking off. Compare this to the loud flapping of pigeons. These birds have small wings for their size, and their takeoffs are always noisy.

When a great horned owl is attacking prey, it never takes its eyes off the target.
At the very last second the owl swings its legs forward to grab the prey.

This hungry snowy owl has caught a gray partridge, a common prey on its wintering grounds in the prairies.

The main diet for most owls is a simple one to remember: small mammals for breakfast, small mammals for lunch, and small mammals for dinner. Favorite mammals include mice, voles, lemmings, chipmunks, tree squirrels, pocket gophers, flying squirrels, pack rats, rabbits, and hares.

A family of snowy owls may feed on 2,600 lemmings in a summer. A hungry great gray owl may consume 1,400 voles in a year. And in its lifetime, an average barn owl may eat as many as 11,000 mice, whiskers and all!

Some of the smallest owls, including the tiny elf owl and the flammulated owl, hardly weigh more than a mouse themselves. These small owls are mainly insect hunters, preying on crickets, spiders, beetles, grasshoppers, and moths.

Owls
FUNFACT:

The great horned owl is the most common owl in the United States and Canada, living in many different areas such as cypress swamps, northern spruce forests, deciduous forests, prairies, mountains, and deserts.

Many owls hunt other birds when they get a chance. In winter, the northern hawk owl often hunts grouse and ptarmigan (TAR-mih-gun), and the fast-flying northern pygmy-owl attacks small songbirds such as juncos, redpolls, and chickadees. In New Jersey, a bold eastern screech owl once flew down the chimney of a house and ate the family's pet canary. It had pulled the unhappy bird through the bars of its cage!

Owls sometimes kill more prey than they can immediately eat. They store the surplus food for later. This is especially common for northern owls in winter. They may be unable to hunt for several days or a week because of blizzards. In these cases the stored food may freeze as hard as wood. Before a small boreal owl or northern saw-whet owl can eat its frozen meal, it must thaw it out. It does this by sitting on its food as if warming an egg.

When prey is plentiful, a northern hawk owl will often store extra food in the hollow ends of old branches and eat it later.

This burrowing owl has caught a meadow vole that is almost as big as itself. The bird is bringing food to its mate, which is nesting underground in the hole on the left.

Many owls also store extra food during the nesting season to help them feed their hungry chicks. They may store the extra food in a hollow tree, under a bush, in an old woodpecker hole, or in their own nest. One great horned owl nest in the Yukon had 12 uneaten snowshoe hares in it. Another horned owl nest in Saskatchewan contained 2 hares and 15 pocket gophers. Researchers who study animals are called biologists (bi-OL-uh-jists). They once examined a snowy owl nest in the Arctic with 26 lemmings stored around the edges.

Of all the owls, the barn owl stores the most for a rainy day. It often piles 30 to 50 voles, mice, and shrews around its nest. The record for a barn owl nest is 189 voles.

Snakes are an easy target for a hungry owl. Barred owls and several species of screech owls catch these reptiles when they can. The eastern screech owls in Texas hunt nine different kinds of snakes. Some great horned owls may attack fairly large snakes, even deadly rattlesnakes. One great horned owl in Florida tackled a 6-foot-long (2-meter-long) indigo snake. The owl won.

The eastern screech owl brings one kind of snake, the slender blindsnake, back to its nest alive! The owl does not eat the tiny snake but lets it go free inside the nest. The snake becomes the owl's housekeeper. It eats the worms, called maggots, that feed on the dead animals the owl stores in its nest.

Biologists were surprised to discover that baby screech owls sharing a nest with a live blindsnake are healthier than baby owls without a snake in their home. The researchers believe when there are many maggots in the nest they gobble up the stored food and the growing owls get less to eat. So the maggot-eating blindsnake is a helpful houseguest.

Owls
FUNFACT:

Female owls are larger and stronger than the males. This may help them keep the eggs warm and defend the nest and chicks better.

Scientists occasionally find a live blindsnake living peacefully in the nest of eastern screech owls.

The outstretched wings of a great gray owl can measure 5 feet (1.5 meters)!
With its wide wings and tail the bird can fly so slowly it almost seems to float.

Biologists know more about the diet of owls than they do about any other part of the birds' lives. The reason for this is simple: pellets. Once or twice a day an owl vomits up a pellet, or a wad of undigested food from its stomach. Owls often swallow their food whole and the pellets contain the leftovers from the bird's last meal that were difficult to digest. Pellets usually consist of small bones, teeth, claws, or insect parts stuck together with bits of fur or feathers.

The pellet of a barn owl is about 1.5 inches (3.8 centimeters) long and as thick as your thumb. Great horned owls regurgitate (re-GER-ji-tate) pellets 3 to 4 inches (7.6 to 10 centimeters) long, and a snowy owl pellet may be almost as big as a hotdog. By examining pellets, scientists can learn what an owl was eating.

Great horned owls that live in forests tend to be dark brown. Those that live in deserts and prairies are usually much lighter in color.

Spring is one of the best times to find and watch owls. This is when they hoot and holler a lot and are busy raising a family. Owls call the loudest and have the greatest number of calls of all birds of prey. The hoot of a great horned owl can be heard 2 to 3 miles (3.2 to 4.8 kilometers) away, and the hoot of a snowy owl, 7 miles (11.3 kilometers) away. Most owls have 6 or 7 different calls, but a long-eared owl has at least 12 different calls, and a barn owl has 15.

Most people think that all owls hoot. Some of the large owls, including the great horned, spotted, barred, and snowy owl, are good hooters. Others whistle or bark, scream and screech, chatter or toot.

Owls
FUNFACT:

Large owls live longer than small owls. The barn owl, snowy, great gray, and great horned owls can live longer than 25 years. The boreal owl and tiny elf owl may live only 4 or 5 years.

Barn owls are one of the owl species that do not hoot. Instead, they make ghostly screams. These large, whitish owls often nest in abandoned houses, old barns, and churches. It's easy to understand how a nervous person might hear screaming around one of these buildings and think the place was haunted by witches or goblins. If one of these pale-colored owls flew overhead in the moonlight, the person might think it was a ghost.

Owls
FUNFACT:

Small songbirds, crows, and jays often gather around a sitting owl and call out loudly. This gathering is called mobbing, and is a way for the birds to drive the dangerous owl away.

The barn owl is sometimes called the sweetheart owl because the feathers around its face are shaped like a heart.

Every owl has its own alarm call to scare away enemies and predators (PRED-uh-torz), which are other animals that eat owls. The most interesting of these calls is the one used by the burrowing owl. As its name suggests, the burrowing owl nests underground.

To keep predators from entering their burrow, adults and chicks make a harsh buzzing sound like that of an angry rattlesnake. Since rattlesnakes commonly use abandoned burrows as a place to hide, the owl's trick is a clever one.

The burrowing owl is a small owl, only 9 inches (23 centimeters) tall. It uses its long legs to run after grasshoppers and crickets.

Owls, especially chicks, also have a special call when they beg for food. It sounds like someone impolitely slurping soup.

The loudest call that an owl makes is normally the one it uses to advertise its territory. The loudest owls are usually males trying to attract a female partner and also frighten other males away. After a male and female get together, they use special, quiet calls to talk to each other when they are courting.

Once two owls mate, they must prepare to raise a family. They first need to find a nest. Most small- and medium-sized owls nest in hollow branches or tree trunks, or in old woodpecker holes. Here they are hidden from predators and sheltered from bad weather.

Several weeks before egg laying begins, a male northern pygmy-owl may show his mate several different nest cavities. She may squeeze inside each of them, or just peak through the entrance hole. In the end, the female chooses which nest the pair will use.

Old stick nests of hawks, ravens, and crows are favorite nest sites for larger owls such as the great horned, spotted, and great gray. Owls may use an old hawk nest several years in a row. They never fix it up or add anything to it, so the nest eventually falls apart and the pair must search for a new one.

The northern spotted owl is the most threatened owl in North America. It lives in western forests, many of which have been cut down for lumber.

While the female burrowing owl warms her eggs underground,
her mate watches for danger above.

The burrowing owl is the only species of owl that nests underground, sometimes at the end of a tunnel 10 feet (3 meters) long. In Florida, these birds often dig their own burrow, but in the prairies they use old burrows dug by foxes, badgers, prairie dogs, skunks, or ground squirrels. These long-legged little owls like to nest in open spaces. When prairie areas are scarce they move into cemeteries, empty fields, and golf courses, or along airport runways. At one golf course in Texas, a researcher found 27 golf balls inside an owl's burrow. The owl had collected the balls when they rolled near its burrow. Perhaps the bird thought they were eggs and it wanted a really big family!

Owls rarely add twigs, grass, or feathers to their nest. Burrowing owls are different. Many of them line their tunnel and nest chamber with dried bits of cattle or horse manure. Biologists think the birds do this to hide their own odor and fool predators such as red foxes, badgers, and long-tailed weasels looking for an easy meal. The manure may also attract dung beetles, which owls, especially chicks, like to eat. When a curious researcher stole the manure to see what would happen, the owls replaced the stinky stuff within two days.

Most owls lay 3 to 6 round, white eggs. The eggs of the tiny elf owl are smaller than a grape. Those of the great horned owl are the size of chicken eggs. When food is scarce, owls lay fewer eggs than when food is plentiful. Voles and lemmings are the main food of snowy and short-eared owls. When these rodents are plentiful, the owls may lay as many as 13 eggs. When the rodents are scarce, the hungry birds may not lay any eggs at all.

When a short-eared owl is threatened by a predator, the bird raises its ear tufts in alarm.

The top of a hollow tree stump is a popular nest site for the great gray owl.
It also uses the old stick nests of ravens and hawks.

All male owls treat their mates like a queen. Several weeks before the female begins to lay eggs, the male starts to hunt for her. He will catch everything she eats for the next several months. The female's job is to sit on the eggs and warm them, called incubation (ink-you-BAY-shun). In northern areas, she must cover the eggs most of the time to keep them warm because the cold weather would freeze them solid.

About five or six times each day, she may leave the eggs for a few minutes to poop, regurgitate a pellet, or preen her feathers. Even after the first chicks hatch, the mother owl stays with her young for one or two weeks to keep the chicks warm. During this time, the father owl hunts for the whole family.

Most birds begin to incubate after all of their eggs are laid. Owls, and many other birds of prey, are different. They begin to incubate after the first or second egg is laid. As a result, the early eggs develop sooner and hatch earlier. The first chick may hatch two weeks before the last one. The earlier chicks are bigger. They beg the loudest and get most of the food, so the smaller chicks often go hungry.

Owls
FUNFACT:

It is rare for owls to feed on dead animals that they have not killed themselves. Dead animals, called carrion (CARE-ee-un), are readily eaten by other birds of prey, including hawks, eagles, and vultures.

When hunting is good, there is plenty of food for the entire family. When it is poor, the smallest chicks may die of starvation. Dead baby owls are often eaten by their mother, or fed to the other chicks. When food is scarce, nothing is wasted.

Owl chicks are full-time eating machines! As they grow, so do their appetites. Often, by the time the oldest chick is two weeks old, the father owl can no longer catch enough food to feed his family. The mother owl then has to hunt as well.

Owls
FUNFACT:

Some winters when voles and lemmings are scarce in the north, owls such as the great gray, snowy, boreal, and northern hawk owls fly to southern Canada and the United States.

Even a large meadow vole is not too much for a great gray owl chick to swallow whole. The chick may swallow the rodent in just two gulps.

These barred owl chicks were born inside a hollow tree.

There's not much for young owls to do in a crowded nest while they wait to be fed by their parents. They nibble on twigs or bits of bark, and play with old feathers and pieces of fur. If they live in an open nest they watch the world around them: a red-tailed hawk circling overhead, a chickadee hopping along a branch, or a leaf floating to the forest floor. Young owls are called owlets. As they grow older they begin to exercise their legs and wings. They stretch, flap, and jump up and down. It will soon be time to leave the family nest.

Owls
FUNFACT:

Both the northern pygmy-owl and ferruginous (feh-ROO-juh-nus) pygmy-owl have two dark spots on the back of their head that look like eyes. These false eyes may fool predators into thinking that the owl is looking at them and prevent an attack.

Most owlets leave the nest when they are four to six weeks old. Some of the smaller owls, such as pygmy-owls, can fly when they leave, although not very well. The larger owls cannot fly at this age, but they can glide on the air currents and climb with their feet and beak.

It is important for owlets to leave the nest as soon as they are strong enough. When they are crowded together in one spot it is easy for a predator, such as a pine marten, black bear, or goshawk, to prey on the whole family. When the owlets leave the nest, they hide by themselves in different places, which makes them more difficult to find.

Even after the owlets leave the nest they are still offered meals by their parents for many more weeks. During this time, the young owls must learn to fly well. Sometimes they crash into bushes or land on a branch and end up hanging upside down.

Once they can fly, they must learn to hunt for themselves. They start with foods that are easy to catch, such as crickets, grasshoppers, and frogs. Later they hunt lizards, birds, and mammals.

Like all owls, northern saw-whets hatch at different times so the chicks vary in size.

The boreal owl is one of the most difficult owls for birdwatchers to see because it is small and hides in thick vegetation during the daytime.

Family life for most owls ends in late summer or early autumn. The owlets gradually spend more and more time alone, and their parents feed them less. One day, they finally leave the family territory and fly away. Some owlets settle close to their parents while others travel far away.

In Ohio, for example, biologists observed two barn owlets from the same family leaving home and heading in opposite directions. One went 600 miles (966 kilometers) north to New Hampshire and the other went 500 miles (805 kilometers) south to Georgia. A young snowy owl, however, holds the record for traveling the farthest from home. It hatched in the Canadian Arctic and ended up in eastern Russia, 5,300 miles (8,533 kilometers) away!

In winter, a dozen or more long-eared owls may roost together at night in the same tree.

A young owl faces many dangers when it leaves home. Some are killed by automobiles when they try to hunt in the grassy areas beside highways. Others fly into power lines and fences. Some are killed by other birds of prey such as eagles and hawks, and even more are killed by other owls.

Many big owls eat little owls. For example, the great horned owl includes eight different owl species in its diet.

The most common reason for the death of young owls, however, is starvation. The first year of life is the most difficult for owlets because they are not very good hunters yet. More than half of them die before their first birthday.

43

When hunting in the open, the northern hawk owl watches continuously for predators.

Today many people enjoy watching owls. For some birdwatchers, the great gray, the boreal, and the northern hawk owl are three of the birds they most want to see.

A hundred years ago, former president Theodore Roosevelt said people should wage war on the great horned owl because it killed ducks. Today, people think differently, and all owls are protected.

To see or hear an owl is a special treat, and one of the great rewards of nature.

Internet Sites

You can find out more interesting information about owls and lots of other wildlife by visiting these Internet sites.

www.adoptabird.org/	Adopt-A-Bird
www.EnchantedLearning.com	Disney Online
www.ggro.org/idhelp.html	Golden Gate Raptor Observatory
www.pbs.org/wnet/nture/exbirds/warriors.html	PBS Online
www.raptor.cvm.umn.edu/	The Raptor Center at the University of Minnesota
http://endangered.fws.gov/kids/index.html	U.S. Fish and Wildlife Service
www.animal.discovery.com	Discovery Channel Online
www.audubon.org	Audubon Society
www.kidsgowild.com	Wildlife Conservation Society
www.nwf.org/kids	National Wildlife Federation
www.tnc.org	The Nature Conservancy
www.worldwildlife.org	World Wildlife Fund